CAKES
by NOAH

GLUTEN FREE BAKING

CHRIS WALING

Cakes by Noah – Gluten Free Baking
First Published in 2020

www.cakesbynoah.com

ISBN 978-1-8380750-0-2

Printed in the UK

Recipes © 2019 by Chris Waling
Photography © 2019 by Chris Waling
Food styling © 2019 by Chris Waling
Book design © 2020 by Samuel Huntington

Contents

My
Story
·····
PAGE 8

Part one
Getting Started
·····
PAGE 12

Part two
The Recipes
·····
PAGE 16

Recipe A-Z   PAGE 18

Part three
Bases and Sauces
·····
PAGE 100

Acknowledgements **104**

_My_ **STORY**

How do you start a cookery book? Do you start with the recipes and let the introduction write itself? Or do you actually start writing it at the beginning and work your way through? Is there a right way of doing something? Whatever the answers, I've decided to start at the beginning...

WHY 'CAKES BY NOAH'? Well, if you are going to make something and you want to stand by your product, and it is something you believe in – put your name by it (or at least Noah's). I'm not sure I started Cakes by Noah to write a recipe book, it might have been in there somewhere, bubbling under. I guess the blog was the first stage of the book, I had these grand ideas of world domination with simple every day cakes that looked and tasted great; and were gluten free. At the time the range on offer in the supermarkets near us was a little underwhelming and tasteless, I was sure I could do better!

Each of the cakes and bakes on offer in store had so many ingredients listed – It was unreal! But most of all, there was nothing for children and nothing that a 2-year-old would want. My overriding memory of the time was going into a small, one man-band tea shop and the only cake on offer was a 'Chocolate & Violet Cake'! Really? Even I wouldn't eat that as an adult! Still, to this day, it's not that easy to find something cake wise for Noah in many tearooms across the country. For adults, yes, the range has indeed much improved, businesses are seeing that there is a growing proportion of the population that are, 'going gluten free', coeliac disease aside.

The hospitality industry doesn't cater well for children with allergies and intolerances. They are mainly targeting the adult population and missing the growing up population that will later become paying guests and customers. They will vote with their tummies! Children, as is our experience of bringing up two, do not want to stand out, they do not want to be different. They want to look like, and, more importantly, want to eat, the same as everyone else. Noah just wants to fit in when it comes to food. If we ever want to eat as a family we often go out of our way, or even without, to make sure Noah can be included. Pizza houses get it right for us more than anywhere else. Missing the children out is a bit of a failure, yet another reason to start baking my own – everyone gets to eat the same thing.

Our biggest success in an out-of-home venue was one of Noah's birthday parties in a soft play centre. The long and short of it was that the venue ensured that ALL the children in the birthday party ate gluten free! It was amazing, I nearly cried – such an act of fantastic service that I've never seen before or since; and I'm convinced that it cost them more than they expected. Every child ate with Noah – no separate meal, no making our own packed lunch to take in, no special order. I was overwhelmed. To the venue's credit, I don't think they understood the value of this generous act – there was no additional charge either.

A WORD ON GLUTEN

I am not about to go through the pros and cons of going gluten free, I am not a health professional and I am not a health guru. We know what we know. I'm a chef by trade and training (of some 30 years). I know what we like, and I know what Noah likes. This recipe book is about some of those cakes and bakes and a few more ideas thrown into the mix. Should you need some advice contact a health professional or contact Coeliac UK.

These recipes are as gluten free as I can make them. There is a lot of debate on 'may contain' - please read the labels and make your own informed decision based on what you know your diet will and will not tolerate. 'May contain' is also 'may not contain' – you decide. We know that Noah has no reaction to those products that state 'may contain'. We also know that if there is not gluten (wheat or barley) physically stated on the ingredients on bought products, they are safe enough for Noah. If, as parents, we are not sure – we won't buy them or order them. With my wide experience as a chef I am able to have a certain amount of knowledge and instinct as to how foods are produced and prepared and whether they will be safe for Noah or not. For now, and until Noah is old enough to make those decisions for himself, we are happy to control his intake this way.

HELPING OTHERS

I started the website, and the social media accounts, to show others the ease of gluten free baking, not as difficult as some may think. Its more about the ability and the imagination of the baker. That sharing my recipes, and the life and times of Noah, would help others in the same or similar predicament. Coeliac Disease is for life – it is not a choice. There is constant vigilance required on reading food labels and educating those friends and family around us to ensure Noah doesn't get 'glutened'. The pain we, and more especially Noah himself, went through, is something we'd rather not repeat if we can help it.

2012 WAS OUR DEFINING YEAR

The year Noah was diagnosed; and the year we changed the way we ate in the house. But it wasn't until a couple of years later that I really started to explore the art of the possible and to share our experiences and baking with the world wide web and social media.

Noah wasn't born with Coeliac Disease. It all began the summer before his 2nd birthday, and we were travelling down the country to catch a ferry to France. The drive was a little eventful to say the least and with the benefit of hindsight, we believe Noah had some sort of tummy bug or infection or had travel sickness – or a concoction of all three. The subsequent holiday was a little hampered by the cooler than expected weather but was otherwise uneventful. We returned home ready to return to work, nursery and school – normality.

Oh, how wrong we were! The following weeks and months were harrowing, frustrating and emotional. It would see us going back and forth to the GP, keeping Noah off nursery with unexplained sickness and diarrhoea. We had no idea what was going on – neither, it would appear, did the GPs. The nursery Noah was at were incredible. I don't think we would have got through this time without the support they showed. We were incredibly lucky – Becky, thank you. Each time we would go to the GP, with Noah screaming the waiting room down in sheer pain, they would palm us off with liquids to make him 'go' when we felt he was struggling, they would then give us stuff to make him 'stop' when things got out of hand. We had no idea where it was all coming from.

There were several occasions when we would go up to Noah, when he was asleep and dread what we might find. He was terribly ill, his tummy was distended, and he looked like a malnourished child. It was heart breaking.

SARAH

It was a dear friend of ours, Sarah, who recommended an osteopath and, as a last resort, we tried. We had nothing to lose. With Noah still screaming in pain, which would subside each time he was ill, we went to our local osteopath. Noah was very poorly all over him and as it turned out, that was the best thing that could have happened. The osteopath took one look and concluded that food was fermenting in his stomach and advised us to cut out wheat and dairy from his diet with immediate effect.

We were close to losing Noah; this visit perhaps saved him.

OUR NEW NORMAL

After just four days Noah returned to us. We had to find the right foods that he would eat, but we got there. A few weeks later we had secured a visit with the health visitor; and ultimately the specialist who would finally diagnose Coeliac Disease. Finally, we could move on. Noah had lost some ground; he was underdeveloped and under the average recommended height and weight for his age. No surprise really as he wasn't absorbing any nutrients and minerals from what he was eating. It was going in and then coming straight back out again.

Part

ONE

Getting Started

Filling your cupboards

STORE CUPBOARD

Eggs are all large and free range – left to reach room temperature to allow for more air in the mixing.

Butter is either unsalted or salted and soft. I'm not fussy; life is too short.

I use normal **caster sugar**, rather than golden, unless otherwise stated. Just because.

I use **Belgian chocolate** for cooking and baking – it just tastes nicer

Flour is obviously *gluten free*. There are several varieties on the market and at varying prices. Some are better than others and all are widely available. Find one that you are comfortable using, or at least you can buy. There are gluten free flour mixes that contain xanthan gum, these do not need any further xanthan gum adding to the recipe.

Oats, the *gluten free* variety. Again, these are readily available. However, caution is advised – know your dietary limits. There are some who advise against eating gluten free oats and those that suggest eating them irregularly. I am no health professional; you should seek advice if unsure.

Food colourings I have found that gel colours, used sparingly, are gluten free bake stable. They are widely available so find one that you can work with. Although black is generally not helpful – it turns kind of grey!

Brown sugar I went with light brown or light brown muscovado – it gives that caramel something in the background taste and isn't overpowering. If your preference is for dark brown – go for it. I wasn't going to be fussy with what type of light brown sugar or which muscovado; it'll depend on what you can buy, locally.

Cocoa Shop bought own brand is OK. For a deeper, richer taste there are other, more select cocoas are on the market. I use Food Thoughts Cocoa a lot.

Mincemeat for when it gets to Christmas – there are plenty of products that do not contain gluten and it's not even listed in the ingredients.

Fruit should be as fresh as you can get it

Dairy products in general can be swapped for *dairy-free* varieties

Muffin/Cupcakes/Fairy Cakes – I am not getting drawn into the debate...a muffin is a cupcake without frosting and a fairy cake has wings!

Coffee of your favourite variety. If you prefer a strong coffee or a decaf, the choice is yours.

Dried fruit soaked for a while before using, it will plump up a little and add some moisture to the cake/bake. It will also lose some of the oil that often is used to coat dried fruit. Helping it become more stable during baking.

Stocking up your kitchen

KITCHEN EQUIPMENT

My oven is electric *fan assisted*. All ovens are different and with age will also have to work harder, so know your own oven!

Temperatures can vary, you may need to adjust accordingly – usually up if the oven is not new.

Electric hand-held whisk – there are several on the market – ours is a little over 20 years old and still going strong (famous last words).

Stand mixer (*not essential*) but they are a great help when it comes to volume and size of the bake.

The branch is optional! The rest we accumulated over time and I made the recipes to fit some-easy-to-get-hold-of tins, bowls, cases and trays.

Part
TWO

The Recipes

THE DIFFICULT PROCESS was choosing which recipes to include. So, there are some of Noah's favourites, some family favourites, some from the blog to recount the story that has been taken; and some new ones – at least for us.

KEEPING IT SIMPLE

With each bake, I try to keep them simple to make and have tried to make the instructions as easy as I can. Baking, and then writing how to make the bake, are worlds apart. I hope you enjoy making them as much as you enjoy eating them! And once you have mastered the bakes, try and experiment. Swap a bit of flour for another flour, swap a butter for margarine or some vegetable oil. After all it's how I arrived at these recipes - be brave.

THE ALCHEMY OF BAKING

I have found gluten free baking to be a bit of a challenge. In some/most instances, it's not as easy as swapping 'normal' flours for gluten free flours - they don't behave the same. Gluten free flour does not contain gluten (funnily enough!). There is nothing there to keep it together, to bind it, to keep its shape. Now I know you can use xanthan gum, but there are further debates on whether the increased use, and intake of this,

can be harmful or not. Another discussion I shall keep out of. I am no scientist – but I have had to develop into something of a baking alchemist. Besides, adding xanthan gum does, if you are not too careful, alter the aftertaste of the product. Too much can, and will, alter the flavour. It makes it 'claggy' - it somehow covers the mouth and the end 'eat' is not favourable. I will only add it in small amounts to pastry and biscuits. I leave it out of cakes and cupcakes; you just don't need it in. Unless it is already an ingredient in the flour mix.

Gluten free flour contains ingredients that, once baked, can dry out the end result. You would think that you put less in? Well, yes and no. If you think about what the flour is made up of, it shouldn't really come as a surprise – rice flour, potato starch, tapioca, maize and buckwheat. Not only do they absorb moisture during cooking, they will also continue to dry out once cooked – gluten free baking, at home at least, will last a fraction of the time compared to shop bought products or 'normal' baking products. I have found that adding in more fat/liquid is also required. Yet another reason that 'going gluten free' isn't always the best solution. The best thing is that gluten free baking doesn't really taste that much different – which is kind of the point. At least it is mine.

Recipe  A-Z

A

Apple Toffee Crumble Pudding	76

B

Baked Chocolate Cheesecake	42
Bakewell Tart	28
Battenberg	92
Blackcurrant Sundaes	60
Bread & Butter Pudding	82

C

Caramel Cake	98
Caramel Sauce	103
Caramel Shortbread	20
Carrot Cake	56
Chocolate & Vanilla Marble Cake	78
Chocolate Cake	68
Chocolate Chip Cookies	80
Chocolate Cupcakes	30
Chocolate Fudge Brownies	22
Chocolate Marmalade Cake	84
Chocolate Peanut Butter Cake	88

Chocolate Profiteroles	52
Chocolate Tiffin	74
Coffee Cake	58
Cornflake Tart	50

F

Flapjacks	26
Fruit Crumble	32
Fruit Scones	62

G

Gingerbread Cake	72
Gluten Free Pastry	102

J

Jam Tarts	48

L

Lemon Slice	64

M

Marzipan & Raspberry Cake	40
Mince Pies	46

O

Oat & Raisin Cookies	86
Orange & Cranberry Bars	90

P

Parkin	36
Pastry	102

R

Rice Crispie Cakes	66
Rich Fruit Cake	90

S

Shortcake Biscuits	70
Shortcake Crumble Squares	96
Sorchertorte	34
Sticky Syrup Traybake	54
Swiss Roll	44

T

Tea Loaf	38

V

Victoria Sponge	24

Noah's favourite

CARAMEL SHORTBREAD

My first recipe is Caramel Shortbread as it is Noah's favourite; and has been for some time. It is also a treat where there are several variations – both 'normal' and gluten free. This is our version made with condensed milk, rather than cream, with little chance of burning the caramel or it not setting and becoming a little too runny.

Makes
12-24 servings

Bake
25-30 mins

Difficulty
Moderate

For the shortbread:
150g rice flour
60g cornflour
1/3 teaspoon xanthan gum
140g butter
80g caster sugar

For the caramel:
120g butter
3 tablespoons golden syrup
120g light brown sugar
A tin of condensed milk
(approximately 390ml)

For the chocolate topping:
170g Belgian milk chocolate
30g white chocolate

For the shortbread:
Preheat the oven to Gas Mark 3/160°C/140°C fan and line a small brownie tray, roughly 27cm x 20cm x 3cm with greaseproof paper.

Start by sifting the two flours and the xanthan gum together and put to one side.

Put the butter and the sugar into a large enough mixing bowl and, using a hand-held electric whisk, beat until light and fluffy; this should take about 2 minutes.

Sift in the dry ingredients and using a metal spoon bring the ingredients together (you may also need to use your hands) to form a ball of dough.

Roll out the dough large enough to cover the base of the prepared baking tray and place in baking tray ready to bake. You may need to smooth the dough out to ensure all the base is covered. Gently prick the surface with a fork to stop it rising during cooking.

Place into the oven on the bottom shelf and bake gently for around 25-30 minutes, or until it is a very light brown.

Remove from the oven and allow to cool in the tray.

For the caramel:
Place the butter, syrup, sugar and condensed milk into a large enough saucepan and warm gently over a low heat on the hob to melt the ingredients, continuing to stir so it doesn't stick or burn. Bring to a slow bubble

(taking care as the liquid is incredibly hot) and continue to heat for about 7-8 minutes until the mixture has thickened. The longer you boil the caramel, the thicker/chewier it gets, once it cools. Pour this over the cooled shortcake base.

For the chocolate topping:
Place another saucepan of water onto the hob to heat – no more than a third full of water - and bring to a gentle bubble. Place the milk chocolate into a heatproof mixing bowl and place on the saucepan – to create a double boiler (also known as a bain-marie) – and slowly melt the chocolate ensuring no water gets into the chocolate. Keep your eye on this and don't let the chocolate sit too long - keep stirring it. Once the chocolate has melted pour this over the cooled caramel and smooth over the surface for an even finish.

Repeat the process again with the white chocolate. Once this has melted use a tablespoon to drizzle it over the milk chocolate to create your desired finish.

Allow to cool for about an hour before you score the surface of the chocolate with a knife. Allow to cool completely and finish by cutting up with a hot knife. You can cut the shortcake into as many or as few pieces as you feel you can get away with – 12 large pieces or 24 small pieces which would be great for a children's party.

The ultimate CHOCOLATE FUDGE BROWNIES

HOW MANY?

Your servings can be as big or as small as you like! As a guide, 12 pieces are about right.

Makes
12 servings

Bake
25-30 mins

Difficulty
Easy

200g dark chocolate, chopped into small pieces
100g milk chocolate, chopped into small pieces
150g soft butter
250g caster sugar
120g gluten free plain flour
3 large eggs
5ml vanilla extract

Pre-heat the oven to Gas Mark 4/180°C/160°C fan and line a baking tray roughly *27cm x 20cm x 3cm* with greaseproof paper.

Begin by melting the chocolate and butter in a heatproof bowl set over a pan of water on the hob. Don't let the bowl touch the water; and let the water come to a gentle simmer. Leave the butter and chocolate to melt gently and stir often to get an even melt. Remove the bowl from the heat once melted and leave to cool a little.

Tip the sugar and the flour into the melted chocolate and butter and beat until fully combined. Add in the eggs and vanilla extract and beat until you have a smooth velvety finish. Pour into the prepared, lined tin.

Place into the heated oven and bake on the lowest shelf for 25-30 minutes.

Remove from the oven and cool. Once cool enough, and for that fudgy, squidgy finish, place in the fridge for at least a couple of hours.

Remove from the fridge and the tin and then cut into the desired number of pieces.

Traditional yet tasty

VICTORIA SPONGE

Makes
12-24 servings

Bake
35-40 mins

Difficulty
Moderate

For the cake:
160g butter, melted
150g sunflower oil
250g caster sugar
270g gluten free self raising flour
1 teaspoon baking powder
5 large eggs
2 teaspoons of vanilla extract

For the filling:
120g soft butter
240g icing sugar
1 tablespoon of cold water
5ml vanilla extract
280g jam – raspberry or strawberry or one of your choice
50g icing sugar

Preheat the oven to Gas Mark 4/180°C/160°C fan and line 2 x 8" (20cm) round sandwich tins with greaseproof paper.

Place all the ingredients for the cake into a large mixing bowl. Then, either using an electric stand mixer or an electric hand whisk, whisk all the ingredients together for about 3 minutes until the mixture is fully combined, smooth and creamy.

Pour equal amounts into the two prepared tins and bake on the bottom shelf of the heated oven for 35-40 minutes or until an inserted skewer comes out clean.

Remove from the oven and allow to cool in the tins before removing and placing the cooked cakes on to a wire rack.

Place the soft butter, icing sugar, vanilla extract and water into a mixing bowl. Then with the back of a spoon combine the mixture before then using an electric whisk. Beat the mixture until fully combined and the mixture is soft, spreadable and pipe-able.

Place one of the cakes on to a cake stand and then either spread the buttercream over the surface of one cake or place it into a piping bag and then pipe rings around the cake to get the desired finish as in the picture. Then cover the other side of the cake with the jam, or pipe/spoon into the gaps to get the buttercream and jam rings.

Decorate with the icing sugar passed through a sieve to give the surface of the cake a light dusting.

LET ME GET MY BEAUTY SLEEP

If you can leave the flapjack overnight (or until the next day!) it will 'mature' a little and taste a little richer. It's something to do with the sugar and the syrup; hygroscopic properties!

FLAPJACKS

After two years' worth of 'clear' blood test results from the dietician, she suggested we try to wean Noah onto gluten free oats. Now I realise not everyone can eat or try oats, but this has become a success as Noah is able to safely digest these, without any adverse effect. The recipe...it's not exactly rocket science, but it is certainly a recipe for everyone to make.

Makes
12 servings

Bake
20-25 mins

Difficulty
Easy

250g butter
130g golden syrup
150g soft brown sugar
450g gluten free oats

Preheat the oven to Gas Mark 4/180°C/160°C fan and line a 27cm x 20cm x 3cm baking tray with greaseproof paper.

In a large saucepan (it will need to hold all the ingredients), over a low heat on the hob, melt the butter, syrup and the sugar. You need to make sure the sugar has dissolved but take care not to burn it.

Then simply remove from the heat and stir in the oats so that they are completely covered in the butter and sugar mix. You could if you wanted to at this point, add in 100g of an additional flavour - dried fruit, chocolate or chopped nuts.

Pour this into your prepared tin and press down well, using the back of a spoon.

Bake in the oven, on the lower shelf for 20-25 minutes.

Allow to cool in the tin before cutting into 12 pieces.

A brilliant

BAKEWELL TART

Makes
15 servings

Bake
45-50 mins

Difficulty
Moderate

For the pastry:
140g cold butter, diced
50g caster sugar
170g gluten free plain flour
40g ground almonds
1/3 teaspoon xanthan gum
1 egg, lightly beaten

For the frangipani:
120g soft butter
90g caster sugar
120g ground almonds
2 eggs

Topping and fillings:
200g raspberry jam
50g sultanas
250g icing sugar
1 teaspoon almond essence
4 glace cherries, halved, for decoration

Preheat the oven to Gas Mark 4/180°C/160°C fan and grease a 7" (18cm) deep loose base flan dish

For the pastry:
Place the dry ingredients and the diced butter into a food processor and blend quickly for no more than a minute to bring the ingredients together to resemble fine breadcrumbs. Alternatively, sift the dry ingredients together and then rub the butter into the mix using your fingers and thumbs. Once you have fine breadcrumbs (if using the food processer tip into a larger bowl) mix in the egg and, using your hands, bring the whole mixture together to form a dough.

It will be a little sticky, but it will come good as you roll and finish.

I have found that there is no need to rest the dough, but if you feel the need you can (especially if the weather is hot!). Otherwise crack on with lightly flouring the kitchen surface, bring the dough into a round form and roll out the pastry to about 3mm thick and then line the flan dish.

Once lined, spread the pastry case with the raspberry jam and scatter over the sultanas, then leave to one side whilst you make the frangipani.

For the frangipani:
Place all the ingredients into a suitable mixing bowl and, using an electric whisk, whisk the ingredients together for about 2-3 minutes until light and fluffy. Then gently cover and evenly spread the frangipani over the jam and sultanas. Place in the oven to bake for 40-50 minutes, or until an inserted skewer comes out clean of the frangipani.

Allow to fully cool before you remove the tart from the flan dish.

To make the icing:
Put the icing sugar into a suitable bowl, add the almond essence and mix very slowly by adding the hot water a tablespoon at a time, until you have a thick pourable 'mass'. And, as I don't do finesse, pour over the tart and allow the icing to seep over the edges. You will need a hot butter knife (dipped in boiling water) in order to spread the mixture over the surface.

Finish off the tart by decorating with the glacé cherries on top.

CHOCOLATE CUPCAKES

Cupcakes are good for almost every occasion and we've had plenty of occasions over the last few years. Visitors coming and going from all corners of the globe(ish)!

Makes
12 servings

Bake
20-25 mins

Difficulty
Moderate

For the cupcakes:
150g butter, melted
130g light brown sugar
140g gluten free self-raising flour
3 eggs
30g cocoa
1 teaspoon vanilla extract

For the buttercream:
180g soft butter
330g icing sugar
30g cocoa
Splash of water
Chocolates for decoration

For the cupcakes:
Preheat the oven to Gas Mark 4/180°C/160°C fan and line a 12-hole muffin tray with your chosen cupcake cases.

Place all the ingredients into a suitable mixing bowl and, using the electric hand-held whisk, whisk all the ingredients together until fully combined and you have a lovely smooth and rich batter.

Spoon equally into the 12 cupcake cases and bake for 20-25 minutes.

Remove from the oven and leave to cool before removing the cupcakes from the tray and putting on a cooling rack to cool.

For the buttercream:
Place all the ingredients into a suitable bowl and bring them together using the back of a spoon and then, using an electric hand-held whisk, beat the mixture until you have a smooth and velvety chocolate buttercream.

Place the buttercream into a piping bag with your chosen nozzle and pipe away; finishing off with your chosen chocolate decorations.

I would suggest you eat these within two days of making, to eat them at their best.

Fabulous

FRUIT CRUMBLE

There are a couple of ways to bake crumble. The traditional way would be to put the fruit into the dish, place the crumble on top and bake. Or, cook the fruit and bake the crumble mix separately and bring it all together. Why? I hear you ask. Well. As I have discovered with gluten free flour, it can be a bit of a devil. Baking the crumble first and allowing the mix to then cool and dry will make the crumble mix, crumbly. When baking the whole dish together, allow the crumble to rest before serving.

Makes
4-6 servings

Bake
35-40 mins

Difficulty
Easy

For the crumble:
100g butter (or dairy free equivalent) cold, diced and straight from the fridge
60g light brown sugar
140g rice flour
60g Pecans – chopped

For the fruit:
600g cooking apples, peeled, cored and sliced
100g blueberries
200g strawberries – stalks removed and cut in half
½ teaspoon cinnamon (optional)

Preheat the oven to Gas 4/180°C/160°C fan.

To make the crumble, place all the crumble ingredients into a food processor and use the 'pulse' setting for about 20 seconds; ensuring all the ingredients resemble a crumble, no less. If you have no processor; using your fingertips, rub the butter into the flour, then add the sugar and chopped pecans.

For the fruit mix, place the ingredients into a large enough bowl and gently bring together with the cinnamon and then tip into the crumble dish, cover with the crumble mix.

Place the dish in the oven and bake for 30 – 40 minutes, until the crumble mix is light brown in colour and the fruit juices have started to break through.

Allow to cool and rest before serving.

Alternatively, once the crumble mix has been mixed in the food processor, place the ingredients onto a baking tray, lined with greaseproof and bake (at the same temperature above) for approximately 10 minutes. Remove from the oven and allow to cool. You'll need to break this baked crumble up, before you can sprinkle it over the fruit mix.

For the fruit; place the prepared fruit, with a splash (40ml) of water, into a large enough saucepan and bring to a gentle simmer, stirring continuously to ensure the mix doesn't stick and burn. Cook for about 10 minutes until the apple has softened. Place the softened (and now nicely coloured) fruit into your serving dish and place the now cooled and cooked crumble mix on top.

To warm through for serving, place the crumble into a warm oven (Gas 3/160c/140c fan) for about 10 – 15 minutes.

A very special

SORCHERTORTE

My version of the classic Sachertorte but with a gluten free twist. And named after a near-miss last time of making the actual Sachertorte for the blog; plus, I have a friend whose name closely resembles this new version! So easily confused.

Contains alcohol

Makes
12 servings

Bake
45-50 mins

Difficulty
Hard

For the cake:
150g dark chocolate, broken into small pieces
50g milk chocolate, broken into small pieces
100g butter
5 eggs, separated
130g caster sugar (split in to a 90g portion and a 40g portion)
1 teaspoon vanilla extract
90g gluten free plain flour

For the filling:
180g raspberry jam
100ml vodka

For the topping/glaze:
200g dark chocolate, broken into small pieces
50g butter
60ml double cream

For the cake:
Preheat the oven to Gas Mark 3/160°C/140°C fan and line the base and sides of an 8" deep sandwich tin with a loose base with greaseproof paper.

Start by melting the milk and dark chocolate with the butter, place a saucepan of water onto the stove to heat – with no more than a third full of water and bring to a gentle bubble. Place the chocolate and butter into a heatproof mixing bowl and place over the saucepan and slowly melt the mix – ensuring no water gets into the chocolate. Once melted, remove from the heat and allow to cool.

In a clean, separate mixing bowl, whisk the egg whites, using the hand-held electric whisk, until light and fluffy and resembles a stiff meringue; because that's what we need to make! Once the whites hold their own (and you can turn the bowl upside down and they don't fall out) continue to whisk and add in a tablespoon of the 90g caster sugar at a time, whisking between each addition until you have used up the sugar and have a stiff meringue.

Then in a separate bowl, whisk (you can use the same whisk beaters to save on washing up) the egg yolks and the vanilla extract with the 40g portion of caster sugar until you have a light and pale mix that has doubled in size and if you lift the whisk up, a 'ribbon' is left in the mixture; otherwise known as 'ribbon stage'.

Pour the chocolate mixture and the flour into the egg yolk mixture and gently mix together. Take a third of the meringue and fold in until fully mixed in with no meringue lumps. Take care not to knock the air out of the meringue – patience is required. Repeat with another third of the meringue and finish with the remaining third.

Gently pour the batter into the prepared tin and bake for 45-50 minutes, or until an inserted skewer comes out clean.

Remove from the oven and allow to cool, before removing from the tin and fully cooling.

To make the chocolate ganache:

Melt the dark chocolate and butter in a bowl over a saucepan of hot water (as previously done for the cake). Once melted, heat the double cream gently over a low heat in a saucepan, don't let it boil, so keep your eye on it! Pour the hot cream into the melted chocolate and whisk gently until you have a smooth topping. Allow to cool long enough for the glaze to become spreadable.

Once the cake is cooled and the ganache is cool enough to spread; use one of those fancy cake level cutters or your own expert eye and cut the cake through the middle horizontally. Place one half onto a plate and using a pastry brush, brush the surface of the cake with half of the vodka and then spread with the raspberry jam. Then brush the other half of the cake and place this on top of the raspberry jam – vodka brushed surface on top.

Pour the cooled glaze over the cake and smooth out over the top and sides with a hot knife or off-set spatula.

Once the surface of the glaze has set, melt the white chocolate – this could be done in a microwave as there is so little of it. Place the white chocolate in a microwavable bowl, in small chunks and microwave on full in short 20 second bursts. Pour the melted chocolate into a piping bag to pipe the text.

Cut and serve and eat within 2 days.

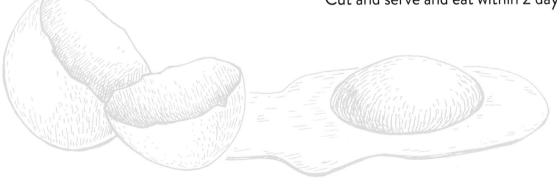

My perfect PARKIN

Normally one for Bonfire Night, I can see no reason why this can't be eaten at any time of the year! And if you can wait, this is best, and I mean best, eaten at least a day after it has been made. Be mindful of your ground ginger – the older it is, the more it loses its taste.

Makes
12 servings

Bake
30-35 mins

Difficulty
Easy

190g gluten free self raising flour
100g gluten free oats
2 teaspoons of ground ginger
100g butter
120g black treacle
100g golden syrup
80g light brown sugar
1 egg

Preheat the oven to Gas Mark 4/180°C/160°C fan and line a cake tin (29cm x 25cm x 3cm) with greaseproof

First, mix the flour, oats, and ground ginger together in a bowl to fully combine them.

Then, put the rest of the ingredients into a large enough saucepan and, over a low heat, gently melt the butter and dissolve the sugar, stirring regularly and taking care to keep the temperature low so as not to boil and burn the sugars, syrups and butter. Remove from the heat once melted, pour in the dry ingredients and mix to combine to a smooth batter then beat in the egg until fully mixed.

Pour into the prepared tin and bake for 30 - 35 minutes, or until an inserted skewer comes out clean.

Leave to completely cool in the tin before removing to slice and if you can, leave overnight to improve the flavour.

A COOL SLICE

Allow to cool in the tin and leave for a day, if you can, before slicing and serving.

TEA LOAF

Another cake that requires a little planning and preparation that can be done the night before. Serve on a rainy afternoon with a cuppa!

Makes	**Bake**	**Difficulty**
10 servings	50-60 mins	Easy

350g dried fruit

200g glacé-halved cherries

1 cup of tea (100ml) made with 1 teabag of your choice (*don't forget to remove the teabag!*)

100g butter

100g caster sugar

200g gluten free self raising flour

2 eggs

Working backwards in time: Place the dried fruit, glacé cherries and tea in a big bowl and mix to combine; then allow the fruit to soak overnight. If you don't remember to do it the night before, then prepare as early as possible in the morning and make the cake in the evening. Allow at least 8 hours to soak.

Once ready to make the cake, preheat the oven to Gas Mark 3/160°C/140°C fan and line a 2lb loaf tin with greaseproof paper.

Drain the liquid from the fruit.

Place the butter and sugar into a large enough mixing bowl then, using a hand-held electric whisk, beat until light and fluffy; then beat in the eggs one at a time until fully beaten in. Fold in the flour and the drained soaked fruit.

If feeling decadent, you could sprinkle some Demerara sugar on top of the cake batter prior to baking.

Pour into the lined tin and bake for 50-60 minutes or until an inserted skewer comes out clean.

Remove from the oven and cool before removing from the tin. Serve on its own, or buttered, and definitely with another cuppa!

Cakes by Noah

39

Marvellous

MARZIPAN & RASPBERRY CAKE

You could possibly make this just after Christmas, around New Year, in order to use up any left-over marzipan. Or just buy some extra marzipan and enjoy! This would be great to serve on a weekend afternoon with friends and glass of something fizzy. I used some chocolate covered marzipan, hence the flecks of chocolate in the cake

Makes
12 servings

Bake
60-70 mins

Difficulty
Moderate

300g marzipan (softened, which can be done with a short 20 second burst in the microwave)
300g butter
6 eggs
2 teaspoons almond essence
250g gluten free self raising flour
200g raspberry jam
100g icing sugar
Pink food colouring
Freeze dried raspberries

Preheat the oven to Gas Mark 4/180°C/160°C fan and line the base of an 8" (20cm) deep cake tin with a loose base with greaseproof paper.

Beat the marzipan and the butter together until light and fluffy; this may take 3-4 minutes. Next beat in the eggs one at a time until fully beaten in. Add in the almond essence and fold in the flour. Mix gently until

you have a lovely batter.

Pour the batter into the prepared cake tin and bake for 60-70 minutes, or until an inserted skewer comes out clean.

Remove from the oven and allow to cool, before removing from the tin.

Once cool enough and using either your expert eye, or the fancy cake cutter, cut the cake in half horizontally.

Spread one half of the cake with the raspberry jam and pop the top back on.

Make the icing by adding a little water and a speck of the pink colouring until you have the thickness required in order to drizzle over the finished cake and then sprinkle over the freeze-dried raspberries.

BAKED CHOCOLATE CHEESECAKE

Rich, luxurious and smooth, with a quick nod to chocolate custard! Although I've flavoured this with vanilla you could easily get away with an orange flavour. I have decorated this for Easter, but feel free to decorate as you please! You could just simply serve on its own, or melt a little chocolate and drizzle it over the surface.

Makes
8 servings

Bake
2h 20 mins

Difficulty
Moderate

For the cheesecake:
200g milk chocolate, broken into small pieces
400g full fat cream cheese
140ml double cream
80g caster sugar
3 eggs

For the base:
250g gluten free chocolate digestives
50g butter, melted

For the base:

Preheat the oven to Gas Mark 6/200°C/180°C fan and line the base of an 8" (20cm) springform cake tin with greaseproof paper. Clearly my tin of choice!

Place the biscuits into a plastic food/sandwich bag and, using a rolling pin, gently bash the biscuits until broken into breadcrumbs. Pour in the melted butter and mix thoroughly, by squeezing and shaking the bag, to cover all the biscuit crumbs with the melted butter.

Tip the buttery biscuit mix into the cake tin, pushing down evenly all the way round and place the base into the oven for about 8 minutes. Once removed, leave to cool whilst making the cheesecake.

For the cheesecake:

Begin by melting the chocolate. Place a saucepan of water onto the stove to heat – with no more than a third full of water and bring to a gentle bubble. Place the chocolate into a heatproof mixing bowl and place over the saucepan. Slowly melt the chocolate – ensuring no water gets into the chocolate. Once melted, remove from the heat and put to one side.

In a separate bowl put in the cream cheese and gently whisk to break it down, then pour in the double cream, sugar and eggs. Beat the mix until fully incorporated, taking care to not over whisk, you only need to mix the ingredients, so this shouldn't take more than a minute or so.

Then quickly pour in the melted chocolate and quickly whisk to combine all the ingredients.

Pour this cheesecake mix onto your prepared biscuit base in the tin and pop in the preheated oven to bake for 10 minutes. Turn the oven down to Gas Mark ½/120°C/110°C fan and continue to bake for about 1hr and 20 minutes, or until the cheesecake has set - no wobble. Turn off the oven and leave the cheesecake in it for at least 45 minutes before fully removing from the oven. Allow to cool at room temperature before finishing off in the fridge to fully set.

Decorate as you wish and, when ready to eat, cut the cheesecake with a hot knife as it will make it easier.

Splendid

SWISS
ROLL

Makes
12 servings

Bake
8-10 mins

Difficulty
Moderate

3 eggs
5ml vanilla extract
80g caster sugar (plus extra for dusting)
80g gluten free plain flour
200g raspberry jam

Preheat the oven to Gas Mark 6/200°C/180°C fan and line a Swiss roll tray (roughly 37cm x 26cm x 2cm) with greaseproof paper

Place the eggs, vanilla extract, and sugar into your mixing bowl and using a hand-held whisk, or the whisk in a stand mixer, whisk the eggs and the sugar on medium speed for about 5-6 minutes. The mixture should quadruple in volume and once whisked should be light and fluffy; if you move the whisk over the top of the mix, it should leave a 'ribbon' imprint.

Sift the flour onto the surface of the egg mixture and gently fold. Using a large metal spoon, stir gently in a figure of eight, up and under, folding gently and slowly to keep as much air in as possible.

Once mixed, pour the batter into the prepared tray, scraping the sides of the bowl clean, and gently smooth the surface of the contents of the tray, before putting it in the oven for about 8-10 minutes.

Whilst this is in the oven, tear another sheet of greaseproof paper, slightly longer than the swiss roll tray, and gently sprinkle

with some extra caster sugar.

Once cooked, remove the tray from the oven, cool for about a minute, before turning the cooling Swiss roll onto the sugar-coated greaseproof paper and carefully peel off the 'baked' greaseproof paper and discard.

Now, depending on how big you want your Swiss roll will depend on where you roll it up! You could go long and thin or short and large. For a long Swiss roll, start rolling from the long edge and using the greaseproof to help you, roll up the Swiss roll, with the greaseproof paper.

You'll need to roll this up quickly after removing from the oven, in order to retain the shape of the result. If you leave it to go cold, it may crack.

Leave the Swiss roll to go cold, before unrolling.

Mix the jam up a bit to make it smooth to spread and starting at the long edge of the Swiss roll, gently spread the jam over the surface of the roll and then gently and tightly (if that's possible!) 'roll' the Swiss roll back up again.

Serve on its own or with cream. You could of course whip some cream up and add this into the Swiss roll before rolling it up! The choice is yours.

Mouth-melting

MINCE PIES

Makes
12 servings

Bake
15-18 mins

Difficulty
Easy

140g cold butter, diced
40g caster sugar
150g gluten free plain flour
½ teaspoon xanthan gum
50g ground almonds
1 egg, lightly beaten
300g mincemeat
Additional beaten egg to finish

Preheat the oven to Gas Mark 6/200°C/180°C fan and lightly grease a 12-hole mince pie tray.

The easiest way to make this pastry is to put all the dry ingredients and the butter into a food processor and blitz the ingredients for about a minute to pulse all the ingredients together to form breadcrumbs.

For ease pour this breadcrumb mix into a large mixing bowl, add the lightly beaten egg and mix together, either with a spoon or get your hands dirty, and bring the mixture together into a lovely dough/pastry ball.

Now, I've found you don't need to leave the pastry to rest, but if you feel the need go ahead. Otherwise sprinkle the surface of your table and your rolling pin with a little flour.

Mould the dough into a ball and gently roll out the pastry to a depth of around 2-3mm in thickness.

Using your cutter, (7cm or 8cm depending on your cake tin) cut out the bases of the mince pies and using your shaped cutter for the top, cut those out too.

Place the base shape into the pastry gently to keep its shape, then once all the bases are in, fill with a level tablespoon of mincemeat, top with your preferred shape, brush them all with the additional beaten egg and sprinkle with an extra pinch of caster sugar.

Place the mince pies into the preheated oven and bake for 15-18 minutes, or until the pastry is golden.

Remove from the oven and leave to cool in the tray before removing and dusting with icing sugar and serving.

JAM TARTS

It's not fair to call this one a recipe!

Makes
Upto 12 servings

Bake
10-12 mins

Cool
1 hour

Difficulty
Easy

Using any of the recipes that use pastry *or the recipe on page 102* simply bring the leftover dough and trimmings together and roll the pastry dough out again; to around 2-3mm in thickness.

Then, using a 7cm round pastry cutter, cut out the rounds, place into your 12-hole tart tray. Gently push the pastry into the mould and then place in a level teaspoon of jam (or curd).

Place into a preheated oven, Gas Mark 6/200°C/180°C fan and bake for 10-12 minutes. Remove from the oven and allow to cool before devouring!

All-time classic

CORNFLAKE TART

An all-time favourite of mine and perhaps one for the older generation; as it appears that Noah has never had this as part of his school dinners!

Part two: The Recipes

50

Makes
12 servings

Bake
30-40 mins

Difficulty
Moderate

For the pastry:
1 x pastry mixture *page 102*

For the topping:
120g raspberry jam
150g gluten free cornflakes
140g golden syrup
50g butter
30g light brown sugar

For the pastry:
Preheat the oven to Gas Mark 5/190°C/170°C fan and prepare a 7" (18cm) deep flan dish with a loose base.

Once you have made the pastry as per the recipe, roll out the pastry to about 3 -4 mm in depth. Make sure you roll out the pastry so that it is wider than the actual flan dish so that it will come up and line the sides.

Line the flan dish and press the pastry gently into the sides. Gently prick the surface with a fork.

Cut out a round piece of greaseproof paper large enough to cover the base. Fill with some baking beans and bake in the preheated oven for 15 minutes (baking blind). Carefully remove the flan from the oven and, with care, remove the greaseproof paper and baking beans from the pastry case. Return the half-baked pastry case to the oven for a further 5-7 minutes to brown the pastry off. Remove from the oven and allow to cool in the flan dish.

Turn the oven up to Gas Mark 7/210°C/190°C fan.

Once the pastry has cooled enough – and keeping the pastry in the flan dish for now, spread the surface of the pastry, evenly, with the raspberry jam.

For the topping:
Place the cornflakes into a large mixing bowl and put to one side.

In a saucepan, gently warm the syrup, butter and sugar until the sugar has dissolved and the butter has melted - you only need to warm this through, no need to boil. Remove from the heat and carefully pour this very hot liquid over the cornflakes, stirring the mixture and cornflakes together until all the flakes are coated in syrup. Turn the coated flakes into the cooked pastry case and press gently to get them all in.

Place the cornflake tart into the hot oven and allow the tart to caramelise for about 8- 10 minutes but do check and ensure it doesn't catch and burn.

Remove from the oven and allow to cool a little and harden, before serving warm with custard or leaving to go cold and enjoy.

HOW MANY?

Makes 15-18 depending on the size of your piping bag hole, but a nozzle around 1-1.5cm should be good.

CHOCOLATE PROFITEROLES

Makes
15-18 servings

Bake
25-30 mins

Difficulty
Hard

For the choux pastry:
120ml water
60g butter
30g gluten free plain flour
50g cornflour
2 eggs

For the chocolate sauce:
180g dark chocolate
150ml double cream

For the filling:
200ml double cream
2 tablespoons of icing sugar

To make the choux pastry:
Preheat the oven to Gas Mark 6/200°C/180°C fan and line a baking tray (roughly 36cm x 27cm) with greaseproof paper.

Heat the water and the butter in a saucepan over a gentle heat on the hob. Keep your eye on it as you only need to melt the butter and have a few bubbles of water. Remove from the heat. There should be enough heat in the saucepan for the next bit to work.

Sift the flours together straight into the water and beat vigorously so that they combine to make a smooth dough. Scrape this mixture into a mixing bowl and have your hand-held electric whisk to hand.

Crack in one of the eggs and whisk the mixture until the egg is fully beaten in; do the same with the second egg. The mixture should become a smooth pipe-able paste.

Pour this mixture into a piping bag with a 1cm nozzle and pipe at least 15 small balls onto your prepared tray. If you are feeling a little professional, use a wet finger and gently press down onto the choux pastry, where you have pulled the piping bag away, to get rid of the little tip.

Place the tray of choux pastry into the hot oven and bake for 20 - 25 minutes, or until bronzed and they come away from the base of the tray easily. Remove from the oven

and allow to cool before placing them on a cooling rack.

Once cold, make a small hole in the base of each profiterole - small enough to get a piping bag nozzle in to pipe in some cream. Put to one side.

To make the chocolate sauce:
Break the chocolate into small pieces and place into a heatproof mixing bowl. Place the cream into a saucepan and heat gently, but do not boil; keep stirring with a spatula so the cream does not catch on the base of the saucepan. Just before the cream comes to a simmer, take straight off the heat and pour over the chocolate. Leave for a minute or two before mixing the mixture together and beating the sauce to a fine, smooth, velvety consistency. Leave to one side.

For the cream:
Whisk the cream and icing sugar in a separate mixing bowl so that it becomes stiff and easy to pipe.

Place the whipped cream into a piping bag, insert the end of the piping bag into the base of a profiterole and fill each one with cream.

Stack the filled profiteroles onto your plate or cake dish and gently pour or spoon over the chocolate sauce.

Superbly squidgy

STICKY SYRUP TRAYBAKE

This is another recipe that has proved popular on the blog over the last couple of years and I've given it a little make over. As with other syrup recipes, if you can bake this one ahead of wanting it - it will improve with time; the syrup just seems to relax and ooze squidgyness.

Makes
12-24 servings

Bake
40-45 mins

Difficulty
Easy

220g golden syrup
120g butter
100g light brown sugar
1 egg
160ml semi-skimmed milk
220g gluten free self raising flour

Preheat the oven the oven to Gas Mark 2/150°C/130°C fan and line a baking tray roughly 25cm x 21cm x 4cm with greaseproof paper.

In a saucepan over a medium heat, gently heat the syrup, butter and sugar, until the sugar has dissolved, and the butter melted, try not to overheat and boil this. Remove from the heat and allow to cool before whisking in the egg and milk. If the mixture is too hot, the egg will scramble, hence why

you need to stop the syrup mixture from boiling. If it does, you'll just have to wait a little while longer before adding the egg and milk.

Add in the flour and beat well until all the flour is completely mixed in, pour into the prepared tin and bake for 40-45 minutes, or until an inserted skewer comes out clean.

Remove from the oven and allow to cool completely before removing from the tin and cutting into squares.

No nuts! just the way we like it...

CARROT CAKE

Makes
8 servings

Bake
50-60 mins

Difficulty
Moderate

For the cake:
3 eggs
150g light brown sugar
50g dark brown sugar
180ml sunflower oil
200g gluten free self raising flour
2 teaspoons cinnamon
1 teaspoon mixed spice
200g grated carrots

140g sultanas (these will need pre-soaking in 4 tablespoons of water the night before, or at least for a few hours beforehand)

For the frosting:
50g very soft butter
100g icing sugar
200g full fat cream cheese
1 teaspoon of vanilla extract

For the cake:
Pre-heat the oven to Gas Mark 3/170°C/150°C fan and line the base of an 8" (20cm) deep round cake tin with greaseproof paper.

In a small mixing bowl, whisk together the eggs, sugar and oil until smooth.

In another mixing bowl, sift together the flour and spices and stir in the grated carrots and pre-soaked sultanas until all the ingredients are coated in the flour mix. Make a well in the middle and add in the egg and oil mixture and stir with a spatula until fully combined.

Pour this batter into the prepared tin and bake for 50-60 minutes, or until an inserted skewer comes out clean.

Remove from the oven and allow to cool completely before removing the cake from the tin.

For the frosting:
Whilst the cake is in the oven, you can start to make the frosting. Simply put all the ingredients into a mixing bowl and whisk together until smooth and fully combined.

Once the cake is cool enough, spread the frosting over the surface of the cake and serve.

COFFEE CAKE

Makes
8 servings

Bake
25-30 mins

Difficulty
Moderate

For the cake:
250g very soft butter
5 eggs
200g light brown sugar
50g dark brown sugar
220g gluten free self raising flour
4 teaspoons of instant coffee, dissolved in 3
teaspoons of hot water and allowed to cool

For the buttercream:
200g soft butter
400g icing sugar
3 teaspoons of instant coffee dissolved in 3
teaspoons of hot water and cooled.

For the cake:
Preheat the oven to Gas Mark
4/180°C/160°C fan and line the bases
of 2 x 8" (20cm) sandwich cake tins with
greaseproof paper.

Place the butter, eggs, sugars and flour in a
large mixing bowl and beat gently until you
have a smooth batter. Pour in the cooled
coffee and stir to mix.

Divide the batter equally between the two
cake tins and bake for 25-30 minutes, or
until an inserted skewer comes out clean.

Remove from the oven and allow to cool
before turning the cakes out of the tins and
cooling completely on a wire rack.

Meanwhile...

For the buttercream:

Put the butter and icing sugar into a large
enough mixing bowl and beat them together
until you have a smooth creamy consistency.
Pour in the coffee and mix again until fully
combined. You may want to add a little water
at this stage if you feel the mixture is too stiff
to pipe. But only add a tablespoon at a time
until you have the right consistency.

Divide the buttercream so that you can fill
the cake, cover the sides and top and to fill a
piping bag ready to decorate.

Beloved

BLACKCURRANT SUNDAES

Here is a little homage to a firm favourite of mine from days of old; and before a well-known high-street clothes and grocery shop changed the recipe.

Makes
12 servings

Bake
25-30 mins

Difficulty
Moderate

For the sponge:
2 eggs
70g caster sugar
65g gluten free plain flour
20g butter, melted

For the pastry:
1 x pastry mixture *page 102*
200g blackcurrant jam

For the buttercream:
60g butter
120g icing sugar
½ teaspoon vanilla extract

For the Genoese style sponge:
Preheat the oven to Gas Mark 4/180°C/160c fan and line a small baking tray, approx. 30cm x 22cm x 2cm with greaseproof paper.

Fill a small saucepan with water to about a third full and bring to a gentle simmer before turning right down. Put the eggs and sugar into a small mixing bowl and place this over the warm water. With an electric whisk, whisk the egg mixture for about 8 minutes over the warm water bath. The mixture should quadruple in volume and after 7-8 minutes should thicken up, so that when you lift the whisk out, it leaves a trail and peak.

Remove from the heat and sift in the gluten free flour. Fold in the flour ever so gently with a metal spoon to ensure you lose no air and the flour mixes in well.

Tip the melted butter down the side of the bowl and fold this in gently too.

Pour into the prepared baking tray and smooth the surface down, gently. Place into the oven and bake for 8-10 minutes. Remove from the oven and allow to cool completely in the tray.

For the pastry:
Once you have made the pastry; keep the oven to the same temperature. Roll out the pastry to about 3mm in thickness; and using an 8cm round, fluted cutter, cut out 12 rounds and place these into a 12-hole tart tin.

When you are ready to cook, place ½ a teaspoon of jam into the centre of the pastry case and then place in the oven to bake for 10-15 minutes. Remove and cool completely before removing from the tin and putting onto a wire rack.

For the buttercream:
Whilst the tarts are in the oven, or whilst cooling, you can start to make the buttercream.

Beat the butter, sugar and vanilla extract together until light, fluffy and easy to pipe.

To assemble: Once the tarts are cool, top up with more jam with an additional teaspoon full, fill your piping bag with the buttercream and pipe a small border of buttercream around the top of the jam and just below the fluted edge of the pastry case.

Using a 5cm round cutter, cut out 12 rounds from the sponge and place these on top of the jam and inside the buttercream pressing down lightly.

They are ready to serve.

Fabulous
FRUIT SCONES *(ish...)*

For me, I had a light bulb moment when making these. As try as I might, replicating the texture of a 'normal' scone was a difficult affair. After all, the flour (the main ingredient) is actually a very different 'flour'. So, a bit like the light bulb moment I had for the profiteroles, I had to think a little differently. So, less rolling for this recipe, more 'dropping'! They still taste great with jam and cream – whichever way around you enjoy them.

Makes
6 servings

Bake
20-25 mins

Difficulty
Easy

250g gluten free self raising flour
40g diced butter
40g caster sugar
100g sultanas/dried fruit
1 egg
80ml milk - approx.

Preheat the oven to Gas Mark 6/200°C/180°C fan and line a flat baking tray; roughly 37cm x 26cm with greaseproof paper.

Place the flour into a large mixing bowl and rub the butter into the flour until it resembles breadcrumbs - or quickly pulse in a food processor for a few seconds.

Stir in the sugar, then make a well in the middle and break in the egg and pour in the milk. Then, using a spoon, stir the mixture together to form a loose dough and then mix in the sultanas. It'll be a little sloppy, but stick with it.

Using a large dessert spoon, scoop the mixture onto the prepared tray, creating 6 dollops of mixture. Space them evenly on the tray so that they bake separately and don't merge during cooking.

Bake for 20-25 minutes, or until an inserted skewer comes out clean.

Allow to cool. These are best eaten on the day but will warm well for the next day as well.

Luxurious
LEMON SLICE

A wonderfully moist and tangy lemon cake thoroughly
enjoyed by our neighbours during testing!

Makes
8-10 servings

Bake
50-60 mins

Difficulty
Easy

240g soft butter
290g caster sugar
4 eggs
220g gluten free self raising flour
Zest and juice of 2 medium sized lemons
50ml milk

Preheat the oven to Gas Mark 4/180°C/160°C fan and line a 2lb loaf tin with greaseproof paper.

In a large mixing bowl, beat the butter and 200g of the caster sugar until light and fluffy, about 4 minutes.

Beat in the eggs, one at a time, ensuring they are fully blended in before adding the next egg. You may need to add a little flour to the mixture with the 3rd or 4th egg so that the mixture does not curdle.

Finish by folding in the remaining flour and the zest of the two lemons. If your mixture is a little thick, you may want to add the milk and even a drop more to give you a 'dropping' consistency to the batter.

Pour the mixture into your prepared tin and bake in the oven for 50-60 minutes or until an inserted skewer comes out clean.

Whist the cake is in the oven, you can make the lemon sugar crust by mixing the remaining 90g of caster sugar with the juice of the two lemons.

Once the cake has finished cooking and is out of the oven, pour over the sugar and lemon juice mix and allow the cake to fully cool before removing from the tin, slicing and serving.

Really easy

RICE CRISPIE CAKES

A quick and easy recipe and great, especially for kids' parties. If you want your cakes to be a little more chocolatey just add more chocolate, but at least you'll know how many crispies to add, which was the key element in creating this recipe!

This will make about 18 rice crispie cakes in the small fairy cake cases.

Makes
18 servings

Difficulty
Easy

240g chocolate
100g gluten free rice crispies

Start off by melting the chocolate in a large mixing bowl. Whilst you can do this in the microwave, heating the chocolate in short bursts of 20-30 seconds, you may get a more consistent melt by melting the chocolate in a heatproof bowl over a pan of gently simmering water. The water must not touch or get into the chocolate and ideally keep stirring until the chocolate has melted.

Remove from the heat and then stir in the rice crispies until they are all covered in chocolate. Then either using a spoon or an ice cream scoop, divide the mixture between the paper cases and allow them to then set before serving.

If you want to, you can decorate the tops of the cakes with your chosen topping, or by covering with extra chocolate!

CHOCOLATE CAKE

Makes
8-10 servings

Bake
50-60 mins

Difficulty
Moderate

For the cake:
250g caster sugar
4 eggs
180ml sunflower oil
100g melted chocolate
210g gluten free self raising flour
40g cocoa
1 teaspoon vanilla extract
1 teaspoon baking powder
50ml boiling water

For the buttercream:
200g soft butter
380g icing sugar
40g cocoa
30ml water

For the cake:
Preheat the oven to Gas Mark 4/180°C/160°C fan and line an 8" (20cm) deep, round cake tin with a loose base with greaseproof paper.

Place all the ingredients for the cake, except the boiling water, into a large mixing bowl and whisk until they are all fully combined, and you have a rich, smooth batter. With the whisk still turning on a low speed, slowly pour in the boiling water and mix until combined.

Pour into the prepared cake tin and bake for 50 - 60 minutes, or until an inserted skewer comes out clean.

Remove from the oven and allow to cool, before removing from the tin and allowing to cool completely.

For the buttercream:
Mix the butter, icing sugar and cocoa together in a large bowl, until all the dry ingredients are combined with the butter, then beat together until you have a rich smooth buttercream. You may want to add the water at the end to get a smoother buttercream that will be easier to spread and use.

Once the cake is cold, cut the cake equally in two horizontally through the middle.

Divide the buttercream into two and use half the mixture to fill your cake, before placing the top half of the cake on, and using the remaining half of the buttercream to cover the cake.

Slice and serve.

Seriously delicious

SHORTCAKE BISCUITS

Depending on the size of your cutter and how you want to decorate your biscuits, this will make approximately 18 biscuits.

Makes
18 servings

Bake
25-30 mins

Difficulty
Moderate

For the shortcake:
180g rice flour
80g cornflour
¼ teaspoon xanthan gun
140g butter
80g caster sugar, plus extra for dusting

Fillings/toppings of choice:
110g melted chocolate plus zest of one orange or;
250g punnet strawberries and a tub of clotted cream

Preheat the oven to Gas Mark 4/180°C/160°C fan and line 2 flat baking trays roughly 37cm x 26cm with greaseproof paper.

Sift the flours and xanthan gum together in a bowl and put to one side.

In a separate mixing bowl beat the butter and sugar together until light and fluffy; about 3-4 minutes.

Tip in the dry ingredients and stir to mix until you have a smooth ball of dough.

In order to roll out the dough place about a 50cm length of cling film onto your work surface, lightly flatten your dough and place this on the cling film, before placing another similar length of cling film over the top of the dough. Using your rolling pin, roll out the dough to about 5-6mm in depth.

Using your cutter of choice, gently cut out your desired shapes and place them onto the prepared trays. You will need to bring the dough back together a couple of times in order to get all your biscuits cut out. Be careful when bringing the dough back together each time you cut out your pieces and try not to be too rough as this will affect

the end biscuit as they will be over-worked and tough.

Once you are ready to bake, lightly dust the biscuits with some additional caster sugar and bake in the oven for 25-30 minutes.

Remove from the oven and allow to fully cool on the tray before removing and placing on a wire rack.

For the toppings:
Depending on your desired finish; mix half the orange zest into the melted chocolate and then dip in the biscuits, placing them onto some greaseproof to allow the chocolate to set and the decorate with the remaining orange zest. You could also put the orange zest into the shortbread at the stage where you add the flour, prior to baking.

If using the strawberries and cream; place a spoon of clotted cream onto each biscuit before scattering with sliced strawberries and topping with another biscuit.

Gorgeous

GINGERBREAD CAKE

Rich and delicious. Enjoyable at any time of the year, especially Autumn and Winter around a bonfire.

Makes
12 servings

Bake
60-70 mins

Difficulty
Moderate

For the gingerbread:
1 egg
300ml milk
400g gluten free plain flour
2 teaspoons ground ginger
1 ½ teaspoons baking powder
180g butter
180g black treacle
180g golden syrup
100g dark brown sugar
80g light brown sugar

For the icing:
300g icing sugar
Water to mix

Preheat the oven to Gas Mark 3/170°C/150°C fan and line the base and sides of a 9" (23cm) square cake tin.

Whisk the egg and milk together in a bowl and put to one side.

Sift the flour, baking powder and ground ginger together and put to one side.

Into a large heavy based saucepan put the butter, syrup, treacle and sugars; and heat over a low heat in order to melt the butter and dissolve the sugars. You only need to melt and dissolve the contents as you then need to allow the mixture to be cool; to touch, before whisking in the egg and milk mixture. Too hot and you will end up cooking the egg before it goes into the oven, and you will end up with bits in your cake! Tip in the flour mix and stir to fully combine the ingredients.

Pour the mixture into the prepared cake tin and bake slowly for 60 - 70 minutes or until an inserted skewer comes out clean. Allow to cool completely in the tin.

Once cooled, you can make the icing. Simply tip the icing into a large enough mixing bowl and by adding a tablespoon of water at a time, make the water icing into a smooth thick paste. Pour over the gingerbread and allow to set before removing from the tin and cutting into squares.

WONDERFULLY EASY

A no-bake recipe which is great for parties, gatherings or just a mid-week treat!

CHOCOLATE TIFFIN

Makes
8-10 servings

Difficulty
Easy

450g chocolate
70g butter
1 tablespoon golden syrup
100g raisins (optional)
145g crushed (but not too much – you are
not looking for breadcrumbs here) gluten
free biscuits/cookies/shortbread

Begin by lining your brownie tin, roughly
27cm x 20cm x 3cm with greaseproof paper.

Put 250g of the chocolate, the butter and
the syrup into a large mixing bowl, and place
this over a saucepan of gently simmering
water, ensuring the water/steam does not
make contact with the contents. Allow the
mixture to melt, stirring occasionally.

Once melted, pour in the raisins if desired
and crushed biscuits; and stir to cover them
in chocolate.

Tip this into your prepared tin and push the
contents into the corners, flatten down and
leave to set.

Once set, melt the remaining 200g of
chocolate, again in a mixing bowl set
over a pan of gently simmering water. Or
alternatively in short, 20 second bursts in the
microwave. Once melted pour the chocolate
on top of the tiffin and smooth out the
chocolate to cover it. Leave this to set for an
hour or so at room temperature.

The topping will not have fully set, so with
a small knife, score the chocolate to divide
it into portions. This will aid cutting the
finished and set tiffin and will ensure the
chocolate doesn't crack and split; giving you
some nice straight lines.

Allow to fully set before cutting into as many
portions as you dare – small or large!

If you must leave this to set in the fridge,
you may notice some white streaks in the
chocolate, this is just the fat in the chocolate
coming to the surface and does not affect
the eating in anyway.

APPLE TOFFEE CRUMBLE PUDDING

Who knew how easy it is to put recipes together? This one kind of sorted itself out.

Makes
6-8 servings

Bake
45-50 mins

Difficulty
Moderate

For the crumble topping:
80g rice flour
80g butter
40g caster sugar
Couple of pinches of cinnamon

For the sponge pudding:
1 tin apple pie filling
3 eggs
150g caster sugar
150g butter
150g gluten free self raising flour

For the toffee sauce:
100g light brown sugar
100g butter
280g double cream

Preheat the oven to Gas Mark 4/180°C/160°C fan and line a baking tray; roughly 37cm x 26cm and a deep baking tray roughly 26cm x 15cm x 4cm with greaseproof paper.

For the crumble topping:
Place all the ingredients into a mixing bowl and, with your fingertips, rub the butter into the dry ingredients to create some breadcrumbs for the crumble topping. You can also do this in a food processor and blitz the ingredients together on the 'pulse' setting in short 3 second bursts to create the same effect.

Tip the crumble mix onto the prepared baking tray and bake in the oven for about 8-12 minutes, or until the crumble has a light brown colouring.

Remove from the oven and allow the crumble mix to cool completely.

For the sponge pudding:
Open the tin of apple pie filling and pour this into the prepared deep baking tin and spread evenly.

Now put the remaining ingredients for the sponge pudding into a large enough mixing bowl and whisk them all together until you have a smooth cake batter, about 2-3 minutes. Pour this over the apple pie filling and smooth out the surface evenly.

Place into the oven (same temperature as the for cooking the crumble mix) and bake for 30-40 minutes or until an inserted skewer comes out clean.

Remove from the oven and allow to cool a little before placing a serving dish over the tin and up-turning the cooked pudding onto a large enough plate. Peel off the greaseproof paper gently, scrapping off any apple mix back onto the pudding.

The crumble mix will need to be gently broken up, before then generously sprinkling over the surface of the apple pie pudding.

For the toffee sauce:
Put the cream, sugar and butter into a heavy bottomed saucepan and slowly melt the butter and dissolve the sugar. Bring to a gentle simmer for a couple of minutes to allow the sauce to thicken a little.

To serve, cut the pudding into portions and serve the toffee sauce in a sauce jug.

CHOCOLATE & VANILLA MARBLE CAKE

Makes
8-10 servings

Bake
50-60 mins

Difficulty
Moderate

For the cake:
240g soft butter
230g caster sugar
5 eggs
1 teaspoon vanilla extract
220g gluten free self raising flour
1 teaspoon baking powder
40g cocoa
30ml milk

For the topping:
200g chocolate
50g butter

Preheat the oven to Gas Mark 4/180°C/160°C fan and line an 8" (20cm) round, loose-based deep cake tin with greaseproof paper.

For the cake:
Apart from the cocoa and the milk, place all the other ingredients into a large mixing bowl and whisk slowly at first to incorporate the ingredients; then turn up the speed to fully whisk them into a smooth and silky cake batter.

Place one half of the batter into a separate mixing bowl along with the cocoa and milk; and continue whisking until you have a rich chocolate cake batter.

To assemble the batter in the tin, put one spoon of each batter alternatively into the prepared cake tin in order to create the marble effect. Then once all the batters have been used up, take a spoon and stir with a final flourish to create some extra marbling effects.

Place into the oven and bake for 50 - 60 minutes, or until an inserted skewer comes out clean. Remove from the oven once cooked and allow to cool in the tin, before turning out and cooling on a wire rack.

For the topping:
Once the cake is out of the oven, you can start to make the topping as per the method for the chocolate topping for the Tiffin *(page 74)*, only this time add and melt the butter with the chocolate as well. Stir occasionally to mix the contents.

Once melted and mixed, pour the chocolate mixture over the surface of the cake and smooth out to cover. Some may drip over the side, which is fine.

NOT ONE FOR BEING
A PERFECTIONIST

I'm sure your baking will look
at lot better than mine when it
comes to marbling the cake!

CHOCOLATE CHIP COOKIES

Smooth and squidgy, these will not last long out of the oven.
In fact, slightly warm, they are amazing (even if I say so myself!)

Makes
21 servings

Bake
8-9 mins

Difficulty
Easy

110g butter
170g light brown sugar
1 egg
1 teaspoon vanilla extract
170g rice flour
180g chocolate chips or chocolate broken up into pieces

Line 3 x large baking trays (roughly 37cm x 26cm) with greaseproof paper.

Place the butter and the sugar into a mixing bowl and whisk together until fully mixed; it'll look like breadcrumbs.

Crack in the egg and the vanilla extract and continue to whisk until light and fluffy.

Tip in the rice flour and stir to mix in completely, then add in the chocolate/chips and continue stirring to mix them evenly through the dough.

Using a tablespoon, scoop out the mixture to the size of a walnut (or around 30g – 35g) and roll into a ball, and place this onto the tray.

Continue until you have at least 21 balls divided between the 3 trays, allowing space for the cookies to spread a little during cooking.

Place the trays of the cookie dough into a fridge for about 10 minutes – roughly the time it takes to preheat the oven to Gas Mark 6/200°C/180°C fan.

Bake the cookies, one tray at a time for 8-9 minutes, no more. Any longer in the oven and you'll just have an average biscuit. Remove from the oven and allow to cool and set before removing from the tray and placing onto a wire rack – if you can leave them that long! They may look a little under done, but cooling will finish off the cooking.

Cakes by Noah

81

BREAD & BUTTER PUDDING

Makes
6-8 servings

Bake
25-30 mins

Difficulty
Easy

6 gluten free brioche buns
40g butter
3 eggs
400ml milk
50g caster sugar
5ml vanilla extract
100g dried fruit

Preheat the oven to Gas Mark 4/180°C/160°C fan and grease a ceramic roasting dish, approximately 24cm x 20cm x 3cm.

Begin by slicing the brioche buns into 6 slices and then butter each slice on one side, then put to one side.

Beat the egg, milk, sugar and vanilla extract until fully combined.

Begin to assemble the pudding by covering the base of the dish with a layer of buttered brioche and sprinkle with half of the dried fruit. Cover this with a second layer of buttered brioche and again sprinkle with

dried fruit.

Give the milk mixture another quick whisk, as some of the sugar may have sunk, and gently pour the mixture all over the buttered brioche. You may find the bread rises above the liquid, so just give it a gentle push so that the brioche absorbs some of the liquid and sinks back down.

Place the dish into the oven and bake for 25-30 minutes.

Remove from the oven and allow to cool before serving. With custard, cream, ice cream or all three!

CHOCOLATE MARMALADE CAKE

Makes
8 servings

Bake
40-50 mins

Difficulty
Easy

For the cake:
160g soft butter
80g caster sugar
50g light brown sugar
3 eggs
50g ground almonds
110g gluten free self raising flour
1 teaspoon of baking powder
30g cocoa
4 tablespoons of marmalade
Splash of milk

For the icing:
2 tablespoons of marmalade
100g icing sugar
Water to mix

For the cake:
Preheat the oven to Gas Mark 4/180°C/160°C fan and line an 8" (20cm) deep, loose-bottomed cake tin.

Place all the ingredients into a large enough mixing bowl and gently whisk the ingredients together to form a lovely velvety cake batter. This should take no more than 2 minutes to mix.

Pour the cake batter into the prepared cake tin and bake for 40 - 50 minutes, or until an inserted skewer comes out clean.

Remove from the oven and allow to cool before removing from the tin.

For the icing:
Mix the marmalade with the icing sugar, adding a little water to get the icing to the correct, thick consistency. Depending on how chunky or not you like your orange pieces, you may want to cut the pieces in half. Gently pour the icing over the cake and allow the icing to set before slicing.

OAT & RAISIN COOKIES

Makes
17 servings

Bake
10-14 mins

Difficulty
Easy

130g rice flour
½ teaspoon cinnamon
80g gluten free oats
100g soft butter
140g caster sugar
40g golden syrup
1 egg
150g raisins

Line three large baking sheets (roughly 37cm x 26cm) with greaseproof paper.

Begin by sifting the cinnamon and flour together in a bowl and then stirring in the oats to combine. Put to one side.

In a large enough mixing bowl, beat the butter, sugar and syrup together until you have a light fluffy batter, this should take no more than a couple of minutes.

Then break the egg into the butter mix and beat until fully combined.

Pour in the flour and oat mix and stir in by hand to fully combine; then fold in the raisins.

Use your hands to form the cookie dough into small balls – scoop out pieces of the dough roughly the size of a walnut, or about 35g, and gently roll.

Place each ball onto a lined greaseproof tray. You should get around 17 balls. Try to spread them out over the 3 trays as they will spread out a little during cooking.

Once all the mixture has been used up, place the trays of cookie dough into the fridge to firm up for about 10 minutes.

Meanwhile preheat the oven to Gas 6/200c/180°c fan.

When ready to cook, place a tray of the cookies into the oven – I would advise to cook one tray at a time for an even bake. They take between 10-12 minutes.

Remove from the oven and allow to cool completely in the tray before removing to finish cooling completely.

...there seems to be a theme
running through the book...?

CHOCOLATE & PEANUT BUTTER CAKE

Makes
8-10 servings

Bake
25-30 mins

Difficulty
Easy

For the cake:
4 eggs
220g gluten free self raising flour
40g cocoa
1 teaspoon baking powder
170g caster sugar
160g sunflower oil

For the filling:
160g icing sugar
100g peanut butter (smooth or crunchy)
50g butter
Water to make is spreadable

For the topping:
180g icing sugar
40g cocoa
100g peanut butter (smooth or crunchy)
50g butter
1 teaspoon vanilla extract

Preheat the oven to Gas Mark 4/180°C/160°C fan and line 2 x 8" (20cm) sandwich cake tins.

For the cake, place all the ingredients into a large enough bowl and whisk together until light and fluffy and fully combined.
Divide the batter between the two cake tins and place in the oven and bake for 25 – 30 minutes, or until an inserted skewer comes out clean. Remove from the oven and allow to cool, before removing from the cake tins and cooling completely.

For the the filling, gently mix the ingredients together before beating with an electric whisk until light and fluffy. Then repeat this using the ingredients for the topping.

Once the cake has cooled spread the filling to sandwich the cakes together and use the topping to cover the sides and top of the cake.

Slice and enjoy.

RICH FRUIT CAKE

Makes
10-15 servings

Bake
1hr 50 mins

Difficulty
Moderate

300g sultanas
300g raisins
300g currants
120ml Marsala wine
200g dark brown sugar
200g melted butter
4 eggs
280g gluten free plain flour
2 teaspoons mixed spice
150g halved glacé cherries

Begin if you can, the day before. Weigh out the currants, sultanas, raisins, half of the dark brown sugar and Marsala wine, mix together and place into a large enough bowl and leave to infuse, for the fruit swell, overnight. Remember to cover.

When you are then ready, double line (sides and base) a 20cm square cake time with a loose base with greaseproof paper. Also cut out a square of greaseproof to cover the cake before it goes into the oven to protect the top.

Preheat the oven to Gas Mark 1/140°C/120°C fan.

Sift the flour and mixed spice together and put to one side.

Place the melted butter, the remaining sugar and the eggs into a large enough bowl and whisk together until nice and smooth. Add in the flour mix and bring together with a spoon/spatula. Then either, tip this into the dried fruit mix, including any liquid or tip the dried fruit into the flour/butter mix (it'll depend on which is in the bigger bowl!) and add the glacé cherries; stir it all up until thoroughly mixed.

Carefully pour this into the prepared cake tin, smooth out and ensure the mix gets into the four corners. Place into the preheated oven, with the square of greaseproof paper on and bake for 1hr and 30mins. Remove the greaseproof square top and then finish baking for about 20 minutes, or until an inserted skewer comes out clean.

Remove from the oven to cool completely before removing from the tin and removing the greaseproof.

Finish cooling and cover as required.

GREAT FOR CHRISTMAS CAKE

make on stir-up Sunday and then feed over the prevailing weeks, just before you cover it with marzipan and icing. Rich and indulgent. I've also left out any nuts and mixed peel. It's just a matter of taste.

BATTENBERG

Let's be honest the easiest way of making a Battenberg Cake is by using a Battenberg cake tin. They are widely available online and easy to use. They do look surprisingly small but hold the volume well.

Makes
8 servings

Bake
15-20 mins

Difficulty
Hard

MARZIPAN

Homemade marzipan can taste so much better than shop bought. But it does depend on your tastes, as shop bought can be nice and sweet and packed full of the sweet taste of almond extract and yellow colouring (if you buy it 'natural'). However, if you are making your own use the freshest of almonds; the older they are the final taste of the marzipan will be a little stale. You can of course slightly roast them for a more rounded and pronounced taste. The same for eggs; the fresher and more organic the eggs, the more yellowed the final colour of the paste will be.

For the marzipan paste:
200g ground almonds
130g icing sugar
70 caster sugar
1 egg + 1 egg yolk
4 teaspoons almond essence

Place the sugars and ground almonds into a bowl and mix well, add in the egg, yolk and almond essence and bring together until it forms a stiff dough. This is easy if you use a paddle beater in a stand mixer on a slow speed.

For the sponge:
3 eggs
170g melted butter
170g caster sugar
160g gluten free self raising flour
1 teaspoon almond essence
Drip of pink food colouring
150g smooth apricot jam

Preheat the oven to Gas Mark 4/180°C/160°C fan, then line the base of the Battenberg cake tin with greaseproof and gently grease the sides with a small amount of butter.

Place all the sponge ingredients (except the colouring) into a bowl and whisk to incorporate and until light and fluffy. About 3 – 4 minutes. Divide the mixture equally by placing one half of the mixture into a separate bowl. Then whisk in the pink colouring until you have the desired colour. Once coloured, place the mixture into 2 of the trays in the Battenberg tin and fill the remaining sections with the other part of the mixture. Smooth down and ensure the mixture gets into the corners; give the tin a gentle tap and place into the oven to cook for approximately 15 to 20 minutes. Or until an inserted skewer comes out clean.

Remove from the oven once cooked and allow to cool. Then, remove from the tin and place onto a wire rack to finish cooling.

Once cooled and ready, roll out the marzipan into a rectangle roughly 30cm wide and 20cm long and to your desired thickness. You may have some marzipan left over.... Heat the apricot jam in the microwave in short 10 second bursts (or in a small saucepan over a gentle heat). You want jam that is easy to spread with a pastry brush. Take care as the jam will be very hot.

Place the rolled marzipan on your kitchen sideboard/table/bench with the longest side going left to right. Using a pastry brush, brush the jam onto a quarter of the rolled marzipan, closest to your left. Next place one piece of the natural coloured sponge onto the jammed marzipan, as a long finger pointing away from you. Brush the 3 sides of this with more apricot jam, then place a pink finger by its side, and brush the 2 visible sides with more jam.

Place a 2nd natural coloured fingered sponge on top of the pink, brush the 3 sides with more jam and place the final pink finger alongside and on top of the natural sponge. Brush 2 sides with apricot jam. You should have a Battenberg chequer box taking shape.

Gently brush any remaining jam onto the rest of the rolled out marzipan. Then using your best cake rolling technique, roll the cake up into the marzipan, ensuring you keep hold of the cake as you roll to keep its shape.

Once rolled, gently press the marzipan into the cake to hold and seal with the jam. Trim the two sides for presentation... and tasting Sprinkle with extra icing sugar to serve if you wish.

ORANGE & CRANBERRY BARS

Makes
8-10 servings

Bake
30-35 mins

Difficulty
Easy

250g soft butter

300g soft brown sugar

3 eggs

1 teaspoon vanilla extract

280g gluten free plain flour

1 teaspoon baking powder

1 teaspoon mixed spice

Zest and juice of 1 orange

150g cranberries (if using frozen, defrost them first)

120g icing sugar (for the finished bake)

Grease and line a baking tray roughly 27cm x 20cm x 3cm. Preheat the oven to Gas Mark 4/180°C/160°C fan.

Sift the flour, mixed spice and baking powder together to fully combine and put to one side.

Beat the butter and sugar until light and fluffy; about 4 minutes. Continue to beat as you add the eggs one at a time, beating well into the mixture. Finish by adding the vanilla extract and a spoonful of flour mix with the 3rd egg.

Fold in the remaining flour mix, the orange zest and the cranberries. Mix gently so as not to crush the cranberries. Pour into the prepared tin and bake for about 30 - 35 minutes or until an inserted skewer comes out clean. Remove from the oven and allow to cool, before removing the cake from the tin and cooling completely on a wire rack.

To make the icing. Mix the juice of the orange – a teaspoon at a time – with the icing sugar until you have a smooth, stiff paste.

Cut the traybake into pieces and drizzle over the finished orange icing

SHORTCAKE CRUMBLE SQUARES

Makes
10-12 servings

Bake
35-40 mins

Difficulty
Moderate

140g butter + extra for greasing the tin
90g caster sugar
1/3rd teaspoon xanthan gum
60g cornflour
180g rice flour
200g strawberry jam (or other similar jam/preserve)

Preheat your oven to Gas 4/180°C/160°C fan and grease a small brownie tin (roughly 27cm x 20cm x 3cm) with a little butter

Start off by mixing and sifting together 150g rice flour, xanthan gum and cornflour so its thoroughly mixed and put to one side.

Place the butter and sugar in a suitable mixing bowl and beat until light and fluffy. Tip in the dry mix and stir to combine into a dough.

Remove 60g of the dough and mix with the 30g of remaining rice flour. Rub the mixture between your fingers in a bowl until it resembles breadcrumbs (the crumble)

Line the base of your prepared tin with the larger amount of shortcake dough. The best way I found of doing this was to break the dough into pieces and place these around the base of the tin. Then using your fingers, the back of a spoon or a small glass tumbler, spread the mixture evenly over the base.

Spread the jam over the top of the mixture, leaving an edge around the base other wise the jam will catch on the sides of the tin and burn. Rather like you would when spreading the tomato sauce on a pizza!

Sprinkle the crumble mixture over the top of the jam and place in the oven to bake for about 35 minutes or until the crumble has turned a light golden brown.

Remove from the oven to cool completely before slicing and serving.

CARAMEL CHEESECAKE CAKE

 Makes
8-10 servings

 Bake
20-30 mins

 Difficulty
Moderate

1 quantity of caramel sauce – *page 103*

180g soft butter
200g light brown sugar
3 eggs
1 teaspoon vanilla essence
180g gluten free self-raising flour
110ml double cream
180g full fat cream cheese
70g of caramel sauce

Preheat the oven to gas 4/180°C/160°C fan and line the bases of 2 x 7" (18cm) sandwich cake tins.

To make the sponge mix beat the sugar and butter together until light an fluffy, then add the eggs one at a time until combined. With the last egg add in the vanilla and a spoon of the flour and continue to beat until the mixture is a smooth batter. Pour in the flour and mix with a spoon until fully combined.

Divide the mixture between the 2 cake tins and place in the oven to bake for 25 – 30 minutes. Or until an inserted skewer comes out clean. Remove from the oven to cool, then remove the cake from the tins to cool

completely before filling and covering.

To make the covering (a no-bake cheesecake) whip together the double cream, cream cheese and 70g of the pre-made caramel sauce for a couple of minutes; until its stiff enough to spread.

When you are ready to put the cake together; you may need to gently warm the caramel sauce up to make it pourable. Pour some of the sauce onto one of the sponges to make the filling and then cover with the other cake. Using a palette knife or similar, cover the cakes' sides and top with the cream cheese frosting and finish off the cake by pouring over the top, the rest of the caramel sauce.

Part

THREE

Bases and Sauces

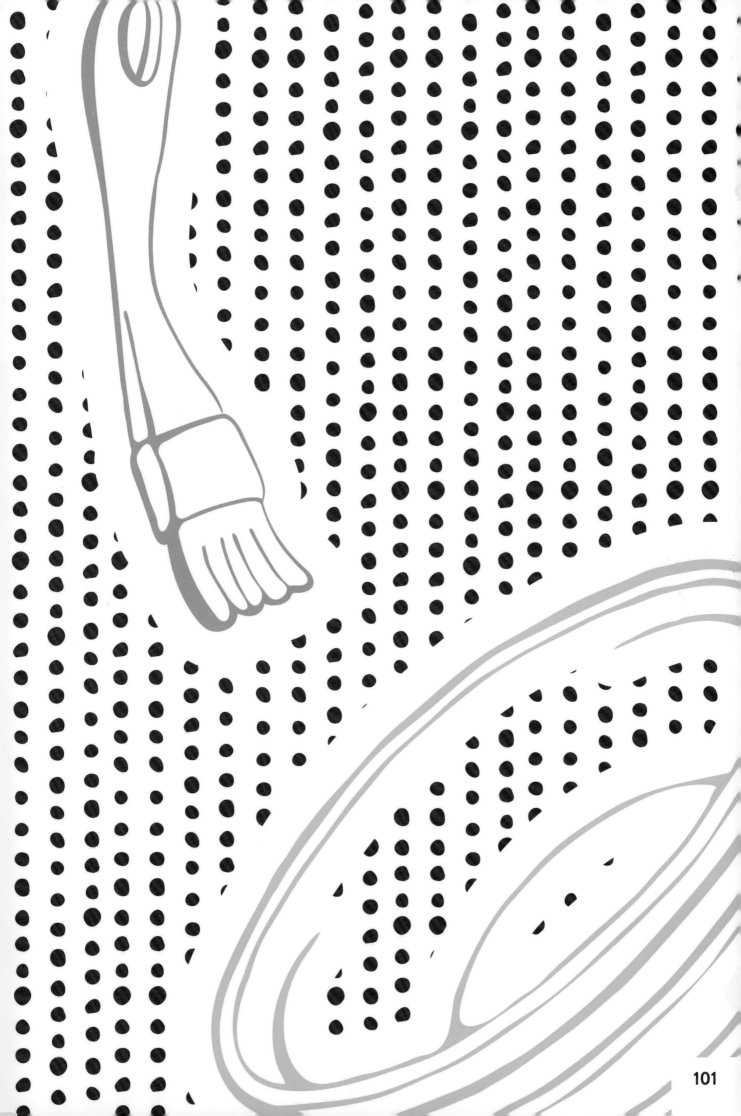

GLUTEN FREE PASTRY

140g butter, diced
200g gluten free plain flour
50g icing sugar
½ level teaspoon xanthan gum (if not
already in the gluten free flour mix)
Cold water to bind – approx. 50ml

Using a food processer gives a quicker result, as you can put the flour, diced butter, sugar and xanthan gum all into the processor and pulse for a few seconds to get the result of fine breadcrumbs. But if you haven't got one, work quickly to rub the butter and flour together to form fine breadcrumbs. Stir in the sugar.

At this stage for both – tip the pulsed mixture into a suitable mixing bowl – then carefully pour in some water to start and using your hands start to bring the dough together.

You may not need all the water, so add this sparingly. You may find that the hotter the weather the less water you need as the butter will be soft enough to bind. Once you have finished the pastry dough, that is slightly tacky, cover with film and place in the fridge until you need it.

CARAMEL SAUCE

220g caster sugar
60ml water
50g butter, diced
150ml double cream
1 teaspoon vanilla essence

You'll need a heavy based saucepan and one large enough to cope with a boiling mixture, plus a pastry brush in a cup of cold water.

Add the sugar and water to the saucepan and stir gently to mix. Then turn on the heat, gently at first to melt the sugar, keep stirring gently. Once melted, turn up the heat to bring the mixture to a gentle boil. Gently swirl the pan to keep the mixture moving in the pan – take care to do this as the mixture in the pan will be incredibly hot at this stage.

As you swirl there will be sugar deposits on the side of the pan; so, carefully using your wet pastry brush, brush the sides of the saucepan to stop the sugar crystallising; place the brush back in the cold cup of water. And repeat as necessary. Keep swirling, brushing and keep your eye on the saucepan.

The mixture should start to colour after around 11 – 15 minutes – dependant on the heat you use. Keep your eye on the sugar as it will turn quickly from a lovely caramel scent and colour to a burnt and bitter caramel within seconds!

As soon as the colour has a gentle amber tone and the scent of caramel, remove it from the heat immediately. Gently add in the butter and whisk until melted – take care as the mixture will 'fizz' up, then gently pour in the cream and vanilla and continue whisking until the mixture turns to a lovely smooth sauce. Leave to cool in the pan before transferring to a tub or jug to use later.

ACKNOWLEDGEMENTS

There are several people to thank.

To my nearest and dearest, my long-suffering other half. It's been at least 5 years to get this point and it was something you suggested I do, almost in the first year I started this whole project! Sometimes you must find your own way to get to the same destination. Thank you, x.

To Iona and Noah, you both are great critics (and a great source of inspiration) You might not have liked everything but what you did like, lasted no time at all. If it didn't last, it didn't make the grade.

Too the many on social media, and I hope you know who you are. Your 'likes', retweets, comments, your encouragement and your invites to various food shows, opening events and baking demonstrations across the country. Thank you. I don't think anyone really understands how much confidence these give. You sit and ponder, create and procrastinate (or even procrastibake!) You have failures and successes and as much as you dare, you share. Continue doing what you are doing, I guess over time you get to work out who to trust and who to take with a pinch of salt.

Recipes, I have tried to be as creative as I can with my recipes. I have tried to be original with the ingredients and the way in which they are put together to create these wonderful gluten free dishes. There are only so many ways to use certain ingredients to create the same cakes and bakes and I have endeavoured to make them my own. Any similarities are coincidental and not designed.

Thank you.